Resilience

Resilience

By Sean Ewing

RESOURCE *Publications* • Eugene, Oregon

RESILIENCE

Copyright © 2024 Sean Ewing. All rights reserved. Except for brief quotations in critical publications or reviews, no part of this book may be reproduced in any manner without prior written permission from the publisher. Write: Permissions, Wipf and Stock Publishers, 199 W. 8th Ave., Suite 3, Eugene, OR 97401.

Resource Publications
An Imprint of Wipf and Stock Publishers
199 W. 8th Ave., Suite 3
Eugene, OR 97401

www.wipfandstock.com

PAPERBACK ISBN: 979-8-3852-3126-3
HARDCOVER ISBN: 979-8-3852-3127-0
EBOOK ISBN: 979-8-3852-3128-7

VERSION NUMBER 101024

Preface

In this collection, the journey unfolds through the valleys and peaks of life, where faith is not merely a belief but an anchor, holding steady through the storms that tear at the edges of our world. These poems reflect the weight of time, grief, and moments when hope seems fragile, yet through every shadow, there is a glimmer of light—a thread of grace woven by God's unwavering hand.

Life often feels like a landscape of brokenness, where we stumble over the jagged stones of sorrow and wrestle with the stillness of a long winter night. Yet even in the darkest seasons, God's love is a presence that lingers—quiet but steady, much like the way an oak tree stands firm in the fiercest winds. In these pages, you'll encounter the depth of human pain but also the resilience that faith brings, the kind of strength that can only be found in Jesus, who entered into our suffering and bore it all.

Each poem invites you into a space where loss and grief are met with the mercy of God. Whether it's the image of a leaf falling, the weight of scars carried, or the silence that follows a storm, these words echo the truth that even in our most vulnerable moments, we are never abandoned. Jesus is there—in the ache, in the struggle, and in the quiet moments when we realize that all the things we've held onto fall away in view of Jesus.

These poems do not shy away from the rawness of doubt, fear, and sorrow, but they point always to the hope that rises in Christ. It is through His grace that we find not only survival but renewal. Whether you are walking through pain, searching for meaning, or seeking a quiet moment of reflection, my hope is that these poems will speak to your heart, reminding you that you are seen, loved, and held by a God who never lets go.

This collection is an offering for those journeying through the complexities of life—those who, in the midst of heartache, are still seeking the light of Christ breaking through the darkness. May you find comfort in the simple truth that it is not the storms, the scars, or the weight of sorrow that define us, but the Savior who carries us through them all.

As you read, I invite you to listen for the still, small voice of God, whispering through the pages. In the midst of grief, in the quiet after the

Preface

storm, may you feel the warmth of His presence and know that you, too, are rooted in His unfailing love and grace. This collection is a companion on the road of faith, reminding you that even in the deepest valleys, God's light is always shining through.

Sean Ewing
September 2024

The Old Oak

There is wisdom in the old oak's stand
bent but never broken, its roots reach deep
anchored in soil thick with storms survived.
Each limb bears the weight of winds long passed
scarred but steadfast, a testament to time
etched in every crease of its bark.

It has seen more winters than I have breath
felt the fire of the sky crack its skin
but still it reaches—upward, skyward, defiant
as if the heavens call it home.
The storms howl, tearing at what remains
but it stands—a monument to grace
that does not yield to the rage of the world.

Grief is like that—silent, unrelenting
its roots dig deep in the heart's dark soil
twisting and growing where we wish it would not.
It wraps around the soul like shadow
weighing down the branches of who we are.
And yet, beneath that weight
something stronger hums beneath the surface.

The old oak has lost limbs to the wind's fury
felt the splitting strike of lightning's touch
yet still it grows, still it stretches toward the light
its roots sinking deeper, year by year.
Grief carves its marks upon us not to destroy
but to remind us of the storms we've endured
the scars we carry like stories written in flesh.

There is beauty in this resilience
the way the oak does not collapse

under the weight of its history
but stands tall, unshaken, its scars a testament
to what remains and what is yet to bloom.
Perhaps grief is like that too
not meant to be forgotten
but carried with a kind of grace.

And beneath the burden of sorrow
there lies something deeper still
a strength, a quiet hope
rooted in the depths of faith.
Like the oak, we reach toward heaven
our hearts lifted by a love unseen
yet ever present.

But beneath the weight of sorrow
there lies something deeper—a strength
that whispers through the cracks
a quiet hope anchored in the roots of faith.
Like the oak, we reach toward heaven
our hearts lifted by the promise of God's love
finding light in what remains
and in the grace that renews what was once broken.

Aging with Grace

It's remarkable how the years slip by
like the soft rustle of autumn leaves
barely noticed until you see the branches thinning
the ground covered with what was once green and full of life.
You don't see it coming, not really
until the mirror offers you a face
that echoes your father's
and your hands, once so sure
feel the weight of things they once held with ease.
But in this slow drift of time, there's a quiet love
like an old leather jacket, soft at the elbows
frayed at the cuffs, but still warm, still yours.
There's comfort in its fit
even as the seams begin to show their age.
You look back, surprised by the weight of what you've gathered
memories, like lures dipped in quiet waters
each one carrying the scent of a different season
blessed by the gentle hand of God.
Nostalgia is a sweet ache, a smile laced with sorrow
but if you linger too long, shadows take root
a reminder that every season ends
and even the strongest trees
will one day bow to the wind.
And yet, I choose not to dwell there today.
Instead, I find joy in the small things
the morning light filtering through the blinds
catching the dust in a slow, swirling dance
seen only if you're still enough to notice.
Or the way the old dog rises to follow
his joints stiff but his loyalty unshaken.
There's a love that grows with age

a deeper grace in seeing the beauty
of what remains, in what God sustains
even as the years slip by.
Aging sneaks up on you
but it brings gifts—the sound of a friend's voice
the feel of earth beneath your boots
the way the world seems to slow
just enough for you to catch up.
And yes, there's a quiet surprise
in finding you're still here, still standing
still able to see the wonder in the everyday
held by the God who's walked beside you all along.
So, I hold onto that—the love and the surprise
letting them fill the spaces where darker thoughts might creep in.
I know they're there, but I choose the light
the light that still shines through the echo of old days
softer now, but no less sweet.

Refined

Lord, fill my heart with your presence, breathe life anew
for I am depleted, a vessel drained and worn.
Instill your vision, a flame that cuts through darkness
dissolving every shadow that seeks to hide your truth.

Lead me through the forge of affliction
mold me in the fire of your love, where purity is formed.
As fate unfolds its decree, ignite within me your divine spark
animating my soul with courage not my own.

I stand unshaken, though the earth trembles beneath me
for what flows within is your strength, unyielding.
Take me, Lord, I am yours—your vessel, your purpose
in your hands, I find my strength, my renewal.

In surrender, there is no loss, only the gain of your grace
a life marked by your presence, guided by your light.
Through the refining fire, let me emerge not diminished, but illuminated
a beacon of love, a testament to your transforming power.

Evening's Fire

There's something about the end of the day, when the sky catches fire
and the sun dips low, painting the world in hues
that feel almost too vibrant, too alive to be real.
You stand there, hands in your pockets, and just watch it unfold
the colors stretching across the horizon l
ike they're reaching for something
you can't quite grasp, as if they're reaching out from God's own hand.

The barbed wire fence runs alongside you
a reminder that boundaries exist
even out here where the land feels endless, where the sky meets the earth
in a line so thin it could disappear if you looked away for too long.
But tonight, you don't look away, you keep your eyes on that fire
on the way the light bends and twists
trying to hold onto the last bit of warmth
before the night takes over. There's a chill in the air

the kind that sneaks up on you, reminds you that summer's grip
is loosening, that the days are getting shorter
the nights a little longer. But you don't mind
not really. There's a beauty in the fading
in the way the light lingers just a moment longer
as if it knows you're watching, as if it's giving you
one last show before it says goodnight.

You could stand here forever, you think
just you and the sunset, the fence and the field
nothing but the sound of the wind and the quiet hum of the world
winding down for the day. It's in these moments
that everything feels clear, that the worries of the day
melt away and all that's left is the peace that comes with knowing
you're right where you're supposed to be—in the hands of God.

As the light fades, you're reminded of His promise
that just as the sun sets, it will rise again
bringing new mercies with the dawn.
The evening whispers of a Creator who paints the sky
who holds the day and night in His hands
who guides you through the fading light
into the assurance of His unending love.

So you stand, and you watch
letting the colors sink into your soul
feeling the presence of something greater
that carries you through the seasons
through the endings and beginnings
through the fire of the sunset and the peace of the night
knowing that in every moment, you are held
guided by a love that never fades.

Awaiting

Death, the old hunter, casts its chilling hand
A shadow lengthening across life's path.
Yet within this cold, life's fragile beauty blooms
A whisper of change rides the relentless wind
Reminding us of breath's brief, fleeting spark
A murmured note in eternity's vast sea.

This life, though vibrant, filled with piercing light
Is but a moment in the endless stream
A single chord in the universe's grand hymn.
Yet death's firm grip falters, its sting softened
For beyond this world lies unblemished life
A realm of endless light, where peace abides.

In Christ, death's power crumbles, cast away
The grave transforms, a gateway, not the end.
Hope roots deep within the hearts that grieve
A promise firm—where tears are gently dried
Where sorrow yields to joy in His pure light
And life eternal waits beyond the veil.

Though death's shadow looms, we fear no night
For in His love, we find our lasting home.
A dawn awaits, where every fear takes flight
Where broken hearts are mended, made whole.
In Christ, the darkness fades to endless day
And life, eternal, lifts us from the grave.

Anguish

In the heart of night, when shadows loom large
I am caught in the grip of doubt
a storm that rages within, relentless and unyielding.
"My God, my God, why have You forsaken me?"
The words spill from my lips, a cry
from the depths of my soul
as I grapple with the void
the silence that drowns out hope.

Faith, once a steady flame, now flickers weak
a fragile thing in the face of this darkness.
I reach out, hands trembling
seeking a touch, a sign, anything
to anchor me in this tempest.
But all I find is the echo of my own voice
a hollow sound that offers no comfort
no reassurance that I am not alone.

Despair closes in, a thick fog
that blurs the line between reality and fear.
I wonder if this is where faith crumbles
where the heart succumbs to the weight
of unanswered prayers and unspoken fears.
Yet, even as the darkness presses in
a sliver of light begins to break through
a faint whisper in the chaos
reminding me of the promises long ago.

With each hesitant step, I inch closer to that light
tentative in my hope, fearful it may vanish with the dawn.
But it does not waver; it grows steadier, stronger
and as I draw nearer, the doubts begin to ease

replaced by a quiet resolve
to trust, to believe, even when the way is unclear.

This is the struggle, the fight to hold on
when all seems lost, when the night is at its darkest.
But it is also the moment when faith is rekindled
not in a blaze of glory, but in the slow, steady burn
of a heart that chooses to believe even in the face of despair.

And in that choosing, I find peace
not the absence of the storm
but the calm within it
knowing that even in silence, God is near
His presence the light that guides me home.

Autumn's Reckoning

Autumn didn't tiptoe in this year, it crashed through the door
a storm rattling windows, bending even the strongest trees
not the gentle release of summer, but a sharp reminder
that nature keeps its own time, unforgiving and abrupt.

Leaves, ripped from branches, fell like torn whispers
leaving trees bare, exposed, caught off guard
as if they too felt the sudden loss, the ache of letting go.

I walked out into the wreckage, where the air turned cold and sharp
the scent of decay replacing summer's warmth.
The ground littered with remnants—each leaf a casualty
of a season that overstayed its welcome
the earth too tired to recover, too beaten down to bounce back.

But in the lull after the storm, a deeper truth settled in.
There's a lesson in the letting go, a grace in surrender
the trees, stripped of glory, stood tall in simplicity
bare branches reaching out, as if in prayer
accepting what had to be, trusting in the unseen.

As I wandered through the aftermath, feeling the weight of loss
I saw the promise in dying, the quiet understanding
that what's taken isn't gone forever, but clearing space for what's to come
trusting that in God's perfect timing, spring will return
renewed, transformed, just as the sun will rise.

So I stand in autumn's reckoning, letting the wind take the last of summer
finding peace in the cycle, knowing God's hand is in it all
guiding us through the seasons, from the harshest storms
to the tender rebirth of spring, always bringing us back to the light.

Split Open

The storm swept through last night
relentless as a force that's long been waiting
leaving the land torn open
Trees split right down the middle, their hearts
laid bare to the heavens, secrets exposed
to winds that carry no answers.
This morning, I stood before the wreckage
staring at a log cleaved clean
its insides raw, unfinished, vulnerable
and in that gash, I saw myself again
split open, the old wound resurfaced
the ache I thought had long been buried.
It was my heart lying there, broken wide
the sap of love gone wrong seeping
into the dirt—sticky remnants of what once was
now feeding only the weeds of regret.
I reached out, fingers trembling, wanting
to press those jagged edges together
mend what the storm had torn apart
but knowing full well
no amount of care or whispered apologies
could make it whole again.
The wood was cold under my hand
and so was I—numb to the ache
yet feeling every splinter as it drove
deep into my soul. This is what it means
to love and to lose
to see something strong and whole
fractured beyond repair
knowing no glue, no tender word
can bring it back to what it once was.

But there's more I know
something that steadies me still
God's faithfulness, a hand that holds
even when the wind howls loudest
even as the storm tears through.
He's there, unmoved, a constant presence
guiding me through the wreckage.
It's that knowing—that quiet assurance
that keeps me standing
when everything around me crumbles.
I walked away, leaving the log to its fate
but not without a seed of hope
taking root in the soil of my heart.
For grief is a storm that rages
a sky that darkens without warning
but through it all, I remain
split open, scarred, yet still standing
waiting not just for the next wind
but for the new life God will bring.
And in the waiting, I hold onto faith
knowing that no matter how hard the wind blows
God's faithfulness will not only carry me through
but will make all things new
in His perfect time.

Beneath a Veil of Sorrow

The sun rises, but it does not rise for me.
Its warmth lost, swallowed by the fog
clinging to my skin, a second layer of despair.
I am shadowed, wrapped in this dark mist
where light falters, where hope itself
is a distant echo, a voice long silenced
by the crushing weight of this world.

I stand alone in this twilight
a figure blurred by the relentless grip of grief.
The colors of life, once vivid, now bled dry
leaving only this dull, suffocating gray.
I reach out, but my hands grasp nothing
seeking solidity where there is none
a ghost wandering among the living.

There is a stone in my chest
rooted deep, growing heavier with each breath
pulling me down into the abyss of sorrow.
The world moves on without me
but I remain here, frozen in time
each moment a cruel reminder
of what I've lost, of what I'll never regain.

Yet, even in this endless night
a spark glimmers, deep within the shadows
a tiny ember of what once was.
I cling to it, fragile as it may be
hoping that one day it will grow
break through the fog, and light the way back.
For now, I am lost, but not yet defeated
not ready to surrender to the darkness.

God's grace whispers in the silence
a promise that the light will return
that the sun will rise again for me.
And so, I wait, in this sacred repose
knowing that His faithfulness
is the spark that will guide me home.
In the return of light, I will find my way
back to life, back to the warmth of His embrace.

For even here, beneath this veil of sorrow
God's love is the light that will break through
turning mourning into joy, and night into day.
I trust in the dawn that His hands will bring
a new beginning, where hope is reborn
and in His presence, I am restored.

Tide

The waves rise, crash, fall, and rise again
bearing the weight of all that's gone
a relentless pull that grips my chest
dragging me deeper into the abyss of alone.
The shore, once my sanctuary
crumbles under the grief I carry
each grain of sand a memory
slipping through fingers grasping for what is lost.

I stand at the edge
my feet sinking into the cold, damp earth
as the ocean breathes its heavy sigh
echoing the emptiness that fills the air.
I strain to hear your voice, your name
but the wind brings only hollow echoes
of a life once lived, now swept away
by the merciless sea of time.

Loneliness crashes over me
a wave that cannot be outrun
its salt seeping into the cracks of my heart
leaving behind the sting of what's been torn apart.
Adrift, a solitary figure on the vast, endless horizon
I search for the shore of what we had
but find only the expanse of what is lost.

Yet, even here, where the sea meets the sky
I wait for the tide to turn, for the waves to recede
for the sun to rise and warm this weary soul.
Though I stand in the shadow of your absence
and the crushing waves of loneliness close in
I remember I am not truly alone.

In faith, I call out through the storm
and find that Jesus is near, His hand
reaching through the darkness, steady and strong
holding me when the tides threaten to pull me under.
His presence a beacon, a lighthouse in the storm
guiding me through the night, whispering
of a dawn that will break, of a day that will come
when these waters will calm, and I'll find rest in His embrace.

The sea may rage, and the waves may rise
but in His love, I find my anchor
in His grace, I find my shore.
For in the ebb and flow of sorrow
there is a peace that transcends the storm
a promise that even in the deepest grief
God's light will find me, His hand will hold me
and I will rise, carried by the tide
of God's unending, unfailing love.

The Weight of Despair

Despair comes quietly, like fog creeping
slipping into the corners of my mind
whispers in my ear as dawn breaks
turning the sun into a cold, indifferent eye.
The morning bears down like a burden
each step a trial, each breath a labor
as if the very earth is pressing down on my chest
crushing me into its depths, an unseen weight
that wraps itself around my ribs, tightening
with every thought of what the day will bring.

The day is akin to picking up a handful of dust
and letting it fall over a grave, and I stand there
watching it settle, feeling the weight of it
on my soul, a quiet burial of joy
a slow sinking into the soil of despair.
I've felt it, the way despair grips
tightens like a vice around my heart
makes me believe that this—this hollow ache
is all there is, that life is just a series of days
spent picking up the pieces, only to watch them
slip through my fingers, falling like dust
over a grave, each fragment of hope lost
to the relentless passage of time.

There are nights when the darkness is thick
when sleep eludes, and the hours stretch long
the pain a constant companion, gnawing
at the edges of my resolve. I wonder then
if the morning will ever come, if the light
will ever find its way through the cracks
in my weary soul. The silence of the night

echoes with the questions I dare not speak
fears that lurk in the shadows of my mind.

Yet in the darkness, there's a flicker
a whisper that refuses to die, a spark
buried deep in the ashes that tells me
this is not the end, that despair is a wave
not the sea, that it comes and goes, ebbs and flows
and if I can just hold on, ride it out
I'll find myself washed ashore, battered but breathing,
with the taste of salt and life on my lips.

I look beyond the smallness, beyond the dust
and the graves, to the sky that stretches wide
to the stars that burn even when I can't see them.
There is more than this, more than the weight
more than the darkness that crowds my vision.
There is light, there is hope, hope in Christ
a promise that transcends the pain
a whisper of grace that speaks of a day
when the sun will warm my face, and the dust
will be just dust—nothing more, nothing less.

And I, I will be free to breathe again
to rise, to live, to see that the wave has passed
and I, I am still here, still standing
still reaching for the sky. For in the midst of all this
God's hand is steady, His love unwavering
and in His time, the morning will break
the weight will lift, and I will find
that even in the darkest valley
His light has been guiding me home.

The path is long, the journey hard
but in every step, there is a grace unseen
a strength that carries me when I can't go on.

For He who promised is faithful
and though I walk through the valley
of the shadow of death, I will fear no evil
for He is with me, His rod and staff
comforting me, leading me to still waters
to green pastures, to the place
where my soul will find its rest.

And so, I press on, through the dust and the pain
through the nights that seem endless
trusting that dawn will come, that the light
will break through, and I will rise
with the strength of the One who holds me
who knows my every sorrow, who lifts
the weight of despair and fills my heart
with the hope of a new day, a new life
a joy that cannot be shaken, even by the darkest night.

Cadillac Flowers

The day descended, heavy with sorrow
the sky bruised and swollen, its clouds weeping
in long, silent streams, as if they too knew
the weight of absence we carried
each drop a tear shed for what was lost.

As we approached the churchyard, the air thickened
with the unspoken grief of those who gathered
each step slower, each breath more labored
as if the earth itself resisted this final farewell.
The Cadillac waited at the curb, black as despair
its engine a low hum, a muted dirge
for all the words we never said, the hugs left ungiven.

Inside, the flowers—orchids, lilies, roses—sat in perfect rows
too perfect for the mess of grief, too neat for the chaos of loss.
They were beautiful, yes, but their beauty
felt like a fragile veneer over the raw wound of goodbye
as if their delicate petals could somehow cushion the blow
of placing our loved one into the ground.

We gathered, cloaked in our finest black
faces drawn tight against the cold, against the rain
that clung to us like a sorrow we couldn't shake.
The casket gleamed, polished wood, rich and warm,
a stark contrast to the earth waiting to embrace it
its depth a reminder of the finality we were forced to accept.

I watched as they lowered it down
the ground claiming what we could no longer hold
a life once so full, now reduced to stillness
a silence so loud it pressed against my chest
until I could hardly breathe.

But even as the flowers were placed—each bloom a final word
the last whisper of color in a world turned gray
I felt the weight of the moment deepen
the realization that this was truly the end of a chapter
that would never be reopened.

Yet, in this finality, a spark of something more
a fragile light of hope, kindled by the faith we shared
by the promises of God that death is not the end
that the grave is not our final resting place
but a doorway to a life eternal, where pain and tears are no more.

We stood there, the rain mingling with our tears
as if the sky itself had come to weep with us
to share in our sorrow, to remind us that even in the darkest moments
we are not alone. The Cadillac waited; its lights dimmed
as if it, too, felt the gravity of the moment, the finality of it all.

And as the earth claimed what was hers
we turned away, leaving the flowers to their slow decay
their beauty fading into the wet soil
a reminder that even in death, there is a beauty
in the way we let go, in the way we remember
in the way we grieve.

For we are held by the hands of God
even as the clouds know too well the sorrow of rain
and in that divine embrace, we find the strength
to face tomorrow, to carry the memory of our loved one forward
to trust that, in the end, it is not goodbye, but see you again.

As we walked away, I felt the weight of loss lighten just a little
knowing that the grave is not the end, but the beginning
of something greater, something more
a life beyond the reach of death, where love endures
in the light of God's eternal promise.

And so, even as we mourn, we do not despair
for we know that in Christ, we have hope
a hope that cannot be extinguished by death
a hope that shines even in the darkest night
guiding us through the valley of grief
leading us to the dawn of resurrection, where joy awaits.

What Remains

Morning breathes softly, light filters through the blinds
a thin veil of sun touching what's left
the knitting abandoned, needles resting like old bones
waiting for hands that have forgotten their purpose.

Magazines, yellowed with time, whisper stories she no longer knows.
Faces, once dear, slip quietly away
memories dulled by the slow decay of a mind once sharp
now softened by years. The phone lies silent
a relic of connection, though she can't recall
who she'd want to reach, or why the voices feel like strangers.

The fan hums a lullaby, stirring the dust
where memories once gathered, now scattered like leaves.
She sits with her tea—its warmth familiar, though the taste eludes her
each morning blending into the next.

Day by day, I watch her slipping further into the mist
her eyes clouded, yet still searching.
Sometimes she looks at me, a flicker of recognition
a spark that fades too quickly, leaving behind
only the shadow of the woman I've always known.

And it's in these moments, the weight of it settles
grief that lingers for someone still here, but not.
I want to pull her back, to remind her of the love
that still surrounds her, but the past is a place
she can no longer visit, and the future a door
she cannot find.

Yet, in the midst of this sorrow, something remains
a faith untouched, a trust in God
that dementia cannot steal. Even when her words falter
there's a peace that radiates from her

like the calm after a storm, knowing she is held
in the hands of her Creator.

She hums hymns she's sung a thousand times
her voice soft, but sure, a melody woven
into the fabric of her being. In those hymns, I find strength
a reminder that grace is enough
even on this painful road.

Sitting by her side, I hold her hand
the warmth of her touch still strong.
The love we share endures beyond the reach of disease
and I pray—not just for healing
but for the courage to walk this path
to cherish the moments we have
no matter how fleeting.

For I know, even as she fades, God's light shines through her
illuminating the path ahead. And through her quiet prayers
her wordless hymns, I find the thread
that ties her to the eternal—a faith that doesn't fade
a love that endures beyond the mind's reach.

As the light of this life dims, what remains is held
in the hands of God—the keeper of her memories
the sustainer of her soul.

The Long Way Home

I'm taking the long way home, like we used to do
when the world was softer, gentler, and you were beside me
your hand in mine—a lifeline in the dark
melting into the comfort of your smile
that tender curve that spoke of love unyielding
a bond I thought was unbreakable, but now feels distant.

The road is lonelier, the miles stretch further
and I reach out for your hand, only to grasp at emptiness
the cold, vacant space where you used to be
lingering just beyond my reach, just out of grasp.
I watch the waves rise and fall on the water
their rhythm a tired heartbeat
mirroring the relentless ache in my chest
the mournful goodbye echoing in the wind.

The sea carries my grief, pulling it from my heart
but the weight remains, anchored deep within
a burden too heavy to bear alone.
So I cast my sorrows into the restless waves
letting them carry my guilt, my endless longing
for the days when your laughter filled my world
when your presence was the music of my soul.

I beg for my heart to be cleansed of this suffering
for the nights to stop screaming your absence
for the void to be filled with more than silence.
I walk this path alone now, the long way home
but it doesn't lead me back to you—
only further into the void, where your name
is the only sound that fills the emptiness.

Yet, even in this pain, I hold on to hope—
that there is a place where grief will end
where the waves will carry me back to you
where your smile will erase the years of sorrow
and we will be whole again, unscarred by time.
But until that day, I will keep walking, keep mourning
keep offering my confessions to the sea
trusting that God's grace will cleanse my soul
even if this wound may never fully heal.

I'm taking the long way home
but home is just a memory
a place where you are, and I am not
a place where the waves whisper your name
and carry my tears to the horizon
to the place where you wait
just out of reach, just beyond my grasp
forever missed, yet cradled in God's unending faithfulness.

Faith Through the Darkness

I've got my faith in you to see it through
but the road is rough, and I stumble, blind
wondering what purpose lies beneath this weight
this endless night that refuses to break.
Each step I take leads me further astray
every destination more phony, more fake
and I'm left here, questioning the path
searching for a sign that this struggle has meaning
that the pain is not in vain, that the tears I shed
are counted, are seen, are known by you.

It's true; don't you know that when you're down
there's only one way to go? But I'm stuck
caught in this mire of doubt and fear
wondering if I'll ever rise again
if your light will pierce this heavy gloom
if I'll find the strength to keep walking
or if I'll fall and fall forevermore.

Can you lift this weight from my shoulder
this burden pressing me into the earth
that burns me from the inside out
leaving my ashes scattered, smoldering
in a pile upon your floor?
I'm burnt, burnt out, burnt up
and I fear that one more gust of wind
will scatter what's left of me
blow me out your door
lost, adrift, a wisp of smoke
in the vast, uncaring void.

But I've got my faith in you to see it through
even when the darkness threatens to consume me

even when the doubts scream louder than the truth.
I hold on, with trembling hands, to your promise
that you are here, that you are working
that somehow, in the midst of this pain
you are crafting something beautiful
something good, something worth the tears and the blood
and the broken dreams that litter my path.

Don't let me blow out your door
don't let me fall too far
for I am weary, I am weak
and all I have left is this fragile faith
this thin thread that ties me to you
this hope that refuses to die
even when the world tells me to let go.
I've got my faith in you to see it through
and though I can't see the end
though the way is dark and the road is long
I will keep walking, keep trusting, keep believing
that you will lift this weight
that you will carry me through
that your hand will guide me to the place
where the light breaks, where the burden lifts
where the ashes give way to new life
and I find, at last, the peace I've been searching for
the peace found only in your mercy and grace.

Tea for One

Without you, my beloved, time unravels
each minute stretching into hours
each day an eternity of emptiness.
I sit here, hands wrapped around a cup
the steam rising like a ghost of what we were
but the warmth does not reach me
it is hollow, like the space you left behind.

Since I have been loving you
the world has slowed to a cruel crawl
each breath a reminder of your absence
each heartbeat a hollow echo
of what once made me whole.
The clock ticks on, relentless and unkind
mocking me with its steady rhythm
its cold indifference to the void you've left.

And now, it's tea for one
a solitary ritual where once we sat together
your laughter the sugar that sweetened the day
your touch the warmth that made life bearable.
But now the table is empty
the chair across from me a silent witness
to the love that lingers in the air
a love that has no place to go.

The days stretch on
each one longer than the last
a parade of moments that mean nothing
without you here to share them.
I pour another cup, but the tea is bitter
a poor substitute for the taste of your lips
for the comfort of your presence.

In death's wake
this slow decay of time
this endless march of hours that refuse to pass
without you, my beloved
the minutes bleed into hours
the days into months
and all I have left is this
a cup of tea, a lonely room
and the ghost of your love haunting every corner of my mind.

It's tea for one
and the silence is deafening
the absence of your voice a wound that will not heal.
I sip the lukewarm brew
and it tastes of sorrow
of all the words left unsaid
of all the time that now stretches before me
empty and cold, a landscape barren without you.

But as I sit
and as I drink
I find a glimmer of light within the darkness.
In whispered prayers, I feel the presence of God's grace
turning the bitter to sweet
as His love fills the empty spaces where you once were.
And though I walk this path alone
I am not forsaken
for in His arms, I find the strength to carry on
to face the dawn that breaks beyond the night.

Anchored in Faith

I long for trust, but it slips through my grasp
grains of sand too fine, too fast
evaporating before they touch the ground.
Tomorrow looms like a shadow
arriving before I can name it
leaving me stranded between breaths
caught in the hesitant stutter of my heartbeat.

The mirror reflects a face blurred by doubt
clouded by the fog of uncertainty.
My eyes search for solidity
but find only the tremble of ghosts
each thought a spider's thread
delicate, unraveling under the weight
of questions that hover, unanswered.

The clock ticks, a steady drip of water
each second a taunt
a reminder that time marches on
indifferent to my uncertainties.
The sun, veiled behind gray curtains
hesitates at the horizon
as if unsure it can rise above this gloom.

And I, cocooned in layers of hesitation
wait for dawn's arrival
not certain it will break
but clinging to the hope
that when it does
it will bring a light I can trust
a certainty that today won't stretch
into the endless echoes of yesterday.

Yet doubt lingers, a ghostly whisper
in the quiet corners of my mind
hinting that maybe, just maybe
tomorrow is the lie I tell myself
to keep breathing, to keep holding on.
But faith—faith is the gift from God
a certainty hidden in the mist
waiting to be claimed
by those who dare to seek it.

In the stillness, I hear His voice
soft yet clear, like the dawn breaking
I am with you, even in this.
Trust not in what you see
but in my unfailing love
the anchor that holds
through every storm.

Rust

Rust, like a slow poison, seeps into the marrow of my days
gnawing away at the shine, turning every hope brittle
fragile as bones left too long in the cold.
It creeps in, a thief in the night, until one morning I wake to find
the weight of it pressing down, a dull ache where joy once danced
with reckless abandon in my soul.

Once polished and bright, I gleamed beneath the sun's embrace
but now, rust finds its way into the hidden chambers of my heart
where dreams once bloomed like wildflowers.
Each trial, each whispered disappointment—another stroke of corrosion
another piece of me crumbling away until the reflection in the glass
is a stranger's, with familiar eyes worn by time's relentless hand.

The world spins on, indifferent to my decay
a machine grinding down the remnants of me
turning flesh to cold metal and metal to dust, scattered by the wind.
I watch, powerless, a witness to my own erosion
wondering if time truly heals or if it is the rust itself
eating away at every hope, leaving me jagged and sharp
a soul guarded, afraid to be touched.

Yet in the quiet wreckage, beneath my worn-out armor
I find more than decay. In the rust, I see beauty
grace unexpected in the scars, a testament to battles fought
a soul that bends but never breaks. Even in the breaking, there is grace
in the way Christ holds me together, a monument not to wear and tear
but to the faith that survives it all.

I stand, reconciled, not by the shine but by the grace
that turns rust to gold, by the love that sees through the decay
to the steadfast soul beneath. In Christ, I find the strength
to bear it all, to stand in the rust and rain, knowing that in the end

when time has claimed what it can, His love will still hold me
whole and free—a testament to the beauty in endurance
to the amazing grace that remains long after the shine is gone.

Rain

The crooked neck of the scraggly oak bends
under the weight of a day gone gray
its twisted limbs clawing at the sky
pleading for a sun long lost
for a warmth it may never know again.

Storm clouds approach, their bellies swollen with the promise of sorrow
displaying a muted gold against winter's palm
a cruel tease of light swallowed by the dusk.

The rain falls like whispered laments, each drop a tiny tear
carving paths of longing down the weeping glass
fracturing the world beyond my window
turning it into a puzzle of half-forgotten dreams.
Inside, the air is thick with the scent of damp earth
of decay that seeps into the bones
as the hours stretch on in suffocating silence.

I watch the world dissolve
the landscape a blur of muted colors
a canvas of gray upon gray upon gray
and feel the weight of it pressing down
heavy as the rain that seems to never cease.
The day drags on, a relentless march of minutes
each one bleeding into the next
leaving behind a trail of weariness
a longing for an end that seems so far away.

But in the distance, a faint light flickers
a memory of something brighter
a glimmer of hope against the dark.
It is small, almost imperceptible
but it is there, waiting to be grasped

a reminder that even in the bleakest of days
faith is worth holding on to.

And so I lift my eyes to that distant light
holding fast to the promise it whispers
knowing that this too shall pass
that the dawn will break the night
and in the light of His grace
I will find the strength to endure.

Renewed

Under the weight of seasons past, the old wheelbarrow sighs
its red paint chipped and rusting, worn by the hands of time.
More than just a tool, it holds stories of labor and love
fields once rich with promise, now quiet under the dust of years.
The rust whispers of days long gone
of earth once turned with hope, now resting in dormancy.

But even in its weariness, there's a quiet strength
a refusal to bend beneath the burden.
The bent frame, the broken wheel
they tell not of surrender, but of battles fought and won.
Each dent a mark of persistence, each crack a testament to resilience.
It lies not in defeat, but in patient endurance
a silent witness to the enduring spirit.

In the fading light of dusk, it speaks of something more
a promise rooted deep in faith.
For in Christ, we are a new creation
not bound by the rust of years
but renewed, made whole in His grace.

Life, despite its fractures, holds a rugged beauty
and beneath the weight of time
there's a strength that does not falter.
In the quiet of the evening
the old wheelbarrow stands as a testament
that even the most battered can endure
can rise again, remade by the hand of the Creator.

In Christ, the scars are not erased but redeemed
each mark a story of grace upon grace.
The wheelbarrow, though worn
carries the seeds of tomorrow

for in His hands, even the old is made new
and every season holds the promise of life.

Mourning

Grief sits heavy, like a stone in my chest
a weight that drags me into the depths
where light struggles to reach
where every breath is a battle
each moment a test of endurance.
The world moves on, but I remain
caught in time's slow grind
waiting for the ache to ease
for the sharp edges of loss to dull
and for the day I can breathe without pain.

A trembling in my bones
a pulse that beats too loud
a rebellion deep within
as if my very being wars with my soul.
In the narrow places where the world shrinks,
sanity teeters on the edge
a fragile balance above the abyss.

Grief comes unbidden and fierce
a shadow wrapping tight around me
clinging like a bitter shroud.
It pulls me down, a weight in my chest
dragging me into the darkness
where lost things whisper their sorrows.
But even here, in the depths
a light begins to seep through
a fragile, trembling joy flutters against the dark
like a moth drawn to the flame.

It speaks of mornings touched by gold
of moments when the world softens
and for a fleeting second, I remember

what it is to be whole.
Understanding carves its way through denial
a slow, painful truth cutting deep.
I search the mirror for the person I used to be
before grief took root, before the world
became something to endure, not embrace.

Acceptance, a bitter pill lodged in my throat
refuses to go down.
But peace comes in broken pieces
a fragile truce sewn with threads of hope.
I wear it like a coat too thin for winter
its seams frayed, yet it holds—just enough
to keep the cold at bay.

So I walk this tightrope
suspended between despair and fragile joy
scribbling down the fragments of light I find
offering them to a world that spins too fast
a world that often leaves me behind.
Yet even in this spinning, I know
God is with me in the grief
His presence a quiet anchor
steadying my soul in the storm.

Through faith, I reemerge
not untouched, but held together
by grace that whispers in the silence
of my darkest nights.
For in the end, His love pulls me back to the light
and I find that even in the deepest grief
there is a way through
a path that leads to hope
a dawn waiting to rise just beyond the shadows.

Pain Walks Back to Me

The sun retreats, warmth fading into the past
and with deliberate steps, darkness encroaches.
Pain, that relentless specter, returns again
resurrecting nights where I was forsaken
abandoned to the cold embrace of despair.

It creeps in like an old, unwelcome guest
settling into the corners of my heart
its fingers trailing icy paths of memory
dragging me into shadows long buried.
There's a weight in my chest, heavy and unyielding
pulling me back into the depths I thought I'd escaped.
Grief overwhelms, a tide that knows no ebb
each wave crashing with the force of what's been lost.
November's chill wraps around my soul
the stars above indifferent, their gaze sharp and cold.
The night is long, and the moon's pale light
offers no comfort, only harsh illumination
of the scars that have not yet healed.

But in this darkness, a spark begins to flicker
a flicker of unyielding resolve that refuses to die.
Memories limp back, draped in sorrow
but I stand firm, refusing to be consumed.
I wander through the labyrinth of my mind
seeking the light, seeking home
knowing that this journey through shadows
is one I must take, but not alone.

For even in this desolation, I am not abandoned.
Christ walks with me, His light piercing the gloom
His hand steadying me when the burden is too great.
The pain persists, the night remains long

but by His grace, I endure.

I rise, not by my power, but by His promise
each step forward a testament to hope reborn.
For in His love, I am held together
a new creation forged in the fires of trial
held secure by the steadfast, unfailing love of God.
And so, even as pain walks back to me
I walk forward, eyes fixed on the dawn
knowing that in Him, the light is sure
and the promise of a new day is certain.

Scars

His only scar, a thin, pale line, etches itself into his shoulder
a remnant of sunburned summers and careless childhood days.
He recounts the tale, practiced—a bike ride gone wrong
a moment of pain now dulled by time.
We laugh, we nod, let the story drift into the past
thinking we understand the weight of what we see.

But scars are deceivers; they hide in the open
cloaked in simplicity, begging no further inquiry.
How often do we miss the fractures
the deep twists and turns beneath the surface?
We see only the healed skin, failing to recognize the depths
the silent stories woven into every thread.

We sit together, sharing words, sharing drinks
but do we truly connect? His eyes, shadowed in the dim light
hold secrets that flicker and fade with every shift.
A tremor in his voice betrays the battles fought alone
the words swallowed before they could wound.

We converse about the weather, about work, about nothing at all
barely touching the depths that lie just beneath.
And I wonder, how many scars do we miss?
How many stories remain untold
buried beneath the forced smiles and laughter too loud, too clear?
What truths do we overlook in the quiet moments
when the world isn't watching?

His only scar—the visible one—is merely a line in the story
a chapter from years long gone. But what of the others, the invisible marks
carved deep into his soul? The ones that haunt his dreams
that twist through his thoughts, weaving themselves into
the very fabric of who he is. How often do we see

but not perceive? Listen, but not hear?
In our ignorance, we leave him to carry the burden
of those unseen scars alone.

We know so little—so painfully little—about those we call close
friends, family, loved ones.
Each of us harbors a world of scars and shadows
of stories half-told, half-concealed, a universe we may never touch
never truly understand.
Yet still, we sit, we talk, we laugh, and in those fleeting moments
we bridge the distance between what is shown
and what is hidden, between the scars we reveal
and those we keep locked away. And perhaps, just perhaps
that fragile connection, that grace-filled patience
is enough to begin the healing.

But there is One who sees it all—every scar, every shadow
and in His love, there is no wound too deep
no story too hidden. Christ, the healer, the redeemer
offers His hand to mend what we cannot see
to bring light into the darkest corners of our souls
turning scars into testimonies of His grace.

In the Silence of Time

I saw a clock the other day, its hands frozen
as if time itself had paused to exhale
a breathless silence, no ticking, no hum
just the cold, deliberate marking of a moment
that stretched too long, filling the empty spaces
between heartbeats, between breaths
that trembled on the edge of being.

I wondered then, what it meant to live
in that breathless stillness
to stand on the precipice of a moment
where time suspends its relentless march
holding me captive in its silent grip.

Time, they say, is why he chose the rope
a silent dialogue, his last words
written in the creak of rope on wood
in the void that swallowed his absence whole.
No letter, no explanation
just the empty, echoing silence
that lingered like a fog in the house he left behind
heavy, suffocating. They whisper it was despair
a needle in the arm, a life not yet begun.

But no, it wasn't love
it was time, the relentless ticking that gnaws at the soul
the seconds that slip like sand through clenched fists
the future always a breath away, just out of reach
always waiting, always there.

I walked down First Street
my steps echoing the rhythm of the clock in my head
that endless beat that drives us forward

even when we want to stop, to linger in the brief, fleeting now
to press pause and hold onto the fragile present.

I met a man, his eyes wild with the rush
the crushing weight of time pushing him down
and I told him the hour, though I knew it didn't matter
four-fifteen, quarter past, the hands on my watch heavy
with the knowledge that time waits for no one
not him, not me, not anyone.

But in that moment, in the thin slice between seconds
there is something more—a breath, a pause
a serenity we almost overlook.
But it's there, it's always there
a whisper from eternity, a gentle nudge
reminding me that even as I rush
even as I chase the ghost of tomorrow
there is purpose here, there is intention in this life
in this God-given moment that time has not yet claimed.

For in the silence between the ticking
in the stillness that God's hand provides
I find that purpose is not in the race
but in the pause, in the breath
in the quiet presence of God
who holds all time in His hands
and whispers to my soul
"Be still, and know that I am God."

Winter's First Kiss

The evening came, hushed and still
when the first snowflakes began to fall
soft as a whisper from heaven's breath
draping the pine boughs in gentle white.
I stood with you, our breath like clouds
watching the fields take on their quilt
each flake a note in winter's quiet hymn.

The air itself seemed to pause
uncertain of this tender gift
and we, like children lost in wonder
marveled at the world made new
each branch and blade touched with frost
the earth beneath us dressed in grace.

I reached out to catch those dancers on the wind
but they melted in my grasp
gone before their beauty was held
leaving only a trace of their dance
a fleeting glimpse of winter's art.

You smiled, that knowing smile
filled with the wisdom of winters past
of nights warmed by a crackling fire
of tales woven from hearth and heart.

And I knew then, as I know now
that this was enough—
to stand beneath the wide, white sky
to feel the first kiss of snow
to be here, together in a world
where God's hand paints the earth with beauty.

The night grew deep, and the snow fell thick

and we, wrapped in our coats, stood in the silence
letting the peace of it all settle around us
content in the moment, content in the knowing
that this was the start of something pure
something that would last—
as long as the snow continued to fall.

The Gift of Time

There's a hush in the air at dusk
when the last light of day leans gently on the earth
and shadows stretch long, like fingers reaching
for what once lay so near at hand.
I tread the familiar path between the pines
a path worn by years of steady steps
each one marking time, each breath a nod
to the seasons that have come and gone.

The years have etched their story on my face
like the rings within an ancient tree
tracing the passage of time with a quiet grace.
I've felt the sun's warm embrace in summer
and winter's sharp bite, cold and clear
but it's in these twilight hours
that time's weight settles most deeply.

With age comes a certain wisdom
a clear-eyed knowing that every moment is a gift
from God, to be savored, not wished away.
The days grow shorter, the nights longer
yet in this dwindling span of time
there's a richness, a depth
that only years can bring.

I pause beside the old stone wall
its edges softened by moss and the touch of memory
and let the moment enfold me.
The wind whispers secrets through the trees
secrets I've learned to hear and hold dear
like the last glow of a fading fire.

Time, I've come to see

is not a foe to be feared
but a companion to be cherished
like an old friend who's walked with me
through valleys and peaks.
Each day, a page in a book that grows thinner
yet more precious with each turn.

So I walk on, slower now
each step a tribute to the years behind me
each breath a prayer of thanks
for what's still to come.
And as night gathers, I hold tight
to the gift of time, knowing that within
its fleeting moments lies the promise
of God's faithfulness, eternal and true.

Sunrise

The dawn arrives slow, deliberate
like a brush dipped in amber and gold
streaking across the sky with patient strokes
each hue a whisper of the Creator's love.

The horizon stretches wide
a canvas ready to bear the weight
of the day's first light
a masterpiece painted anew
by hands that shaped the heavens.

In the quiet before the world stirs
a holy hush lingers
the earth holds its breath
grateful for the gift of another sunrise
knowing what a blessing it is
to see the light unfold once more.

And I stand, a humble witness
small beneath this vast expanse
yet my heart swells with gratitude
for each sunrise speaks of more
than just the dawn of day
it's a testament to God's mercy
a fresh canvas of grace
where shadows retreat
and light proclaims His faithfulness.

This dawn, like every dawn before it
calls me to start anew
to walk in the light He provides
to see His hand in every stroke
and to cherish the art of each beginning
the masterpiece that is every dawn.

Summer's Enchantment

I walk down the quiet lane, searching for the moon
and there it is, faithful as ever
rising to greet the summer night
a golden orb, held in the arms of branches
spilling its light like a promise kept
a beacon of God's enduring grace.

The lane is still, emptied of children's laughter
no dogs pulling at their leashes
only the soft hum of crickets, the flicker of light
from windows half-closed, and the glow
of screens where life moves on indoors.
Yet here, in this hush, I sense His presence.
Fireflies gather, their dance over the grass
an invitation to remember.

I reach out, not for the jar of childhood
but for the memory it holds—those nights
when the world was wide and open
and we lingered under the stars until the streetlights
called us home, the leaves whispering
secrets to the night air, as if they knew
the hand that placed each star in the sky.

Back then, I knew my place—summer's spell
loosening something wild within me
the moon guiding my steps, as if it knew
the yearnings of my restless heart.
Those nights, woven with laughter and light
spoke of a world vast and uncharted
a promise of paths yet untrodden
all under the watchful eye of the Creator.

Now, standing beneath the moon's gentle gaze
its light wraps around me like an old companion.
The fireflies, the breeze soft against my skin
whisper of a truth deeper than memory
that I am still part of this divine magic
still bound to the night
still dancing through summer's warmth
under the care of the One who made it all.

The summer moon, it whispers of freedom
of joy found in the quiet places
guiding me through the shadows
reminding me of the light that has always been mine
not just of the summer
but of the One who placed it in the sky
a steady hand on my path,
a gentle reminder of who I am
in the light of His grace.

Twilight Journey

The road unfurls beneath the evening's shade
a quiet thread winding through the deepening dark.
An old fence stands sentinel, worn by years
holding back fields where shadows now stretch wide.

The sun sinks low, setting the horizon aflame
a brief blaze of orange and pink
before the night draws its curtain across the sky.
This path, well-trodden and known by heart
bears the weight of many wanderings
each step a story, a whispered prayer.
The world seems to pause here
caught between the day's last breath
and the night's first sigh
between what was and what's to come.

I walk this way often
seeking solace found in solitude
a quiet that speaks louder than any voice.
There's truth in how the light
clings to the earth's edge
a soft reminder that each ending holds a new beginning
that every sunset carries the hope of dawn
a promise from the hand of God.

The fence runs true
marking boundaries, charting choices made
yet beyond it, the fields stretch open wide
the sky above vast, unbound
a canvas waiting for the stars to speak of His glory.

And so, I walk, letting the night embrace me
each step a reflection

each breath a quiet thanks for the fading light.
Here, on this road, beneath this sky
I find the peace that eludes me in busier hours
a moment held in the hand of time
where the world is both immense and close
and I, a simple traveler
guided by God's hand, passing through.

Grace in the Seasons

The years have carved themselves deep into my bones
etched by the winds that whisper through the pines
a testament to storms weathered, and soft rains
that washed the earth clean, smoothing the rough edges of time.
I've walked long enough to hear the forest's hum at dawn
to know the rhythm of its pulse, steady in His hand.

There's a resolve that comes only after many summer
when the days stretch long but the years fold in
like a well-worn book, each chapter
etched in memory, written by His grace.

I've seen the fields turn gold, then fall to frost
only to rise again, stubborn and green
death and rebirth, all in His steady gaze.
There's comfort in knowing the world spins on
indifferent to the passing of a single soul
yet each soul held dear in His sight.

In these quieter moments, I treasure the fleeting
the bite of winter's wind on my skin
the way autumn sunlight lingers, hesitant
on the edge of evening, as if it too feels
the weight of running out of time.

Each breath now feels like a gift
each dawn a whispered blessing
and I find myself holding on to the small things
the creak of floorboards in the old cabin
wood smoke curling into a starry sky
the way a dog settles at my feet with a sigh
that speaks of contentment words cannot touch.

I've made my peace with time's slow theft

its trade of youth for wisdom, of vigor for rest.
For there's grace in the letting go, in knowing
what remains is enough—each moment
a thread in the tapestry of a life well lived
woven by His hand.

Now, I walk this path with steady steps
grateful for the light that filters through
the canopy of years, knowing the road ahead is shorter
and that's alright. For I have stood
at the edge of winter's breath
felt the soil crumble beneath my steps
and known the quiet joy of standing still
in this moment, held by grace
as the seasons turn and His light leads me home.

The Path

The path winds through the woods, where roots twist beneath my feet
each step steady, the earth whispering beneath me
a conversation of soil and soul, the trees bending low
as if to hear the secrets I carry. The pines stand tall
their roots deep in the soil of time, like faith anchored and sure
their branches reaching to touch the wind, unbroken, enduring.
Here, the world feels whole, the sky a dome of endless blue
painted by a hand that knows both the grace of light
and the weight of shadow—where His presence settles softly.

I follow this narrow trail cut through green and gold
the land rising like a hymn beneath my feet.
The horizon waits, patient, a distant promise
that I will reach it in time, as He guides each step
steady, sure, as constant as the breath of the forest itself.

The forest breathes with a rhythm older than memory
its pulse woven into the roots, a song sung long before I was
and long after I will be—a testament to His eternal love
ever-present, ever-true, always.

I think of those who have walked this way before
their footsteps now part of the soil, their stories
held in the bark of trees, in the rustle of leaves.
And still, they linger here, their prayers rising
like the curve of branches, always reaching toward the sky.

Beyond the bend, the river sings—a low murmur
of waters winding their own way through stone
their cool breath on my skin a whispered reminder
of the Living Water that sustains, always flowing
always renewing what is broken, what is worn.

I walk on, knowing this path is not mine alone
but shared by all who have come this way—guided by His light.
We pause to feel the same earth beneath us, to marvel
at the same sky, to follow the road that leads
to a place we have always known, yet only now discover
where His grace meets us, where every step finds its home.

Cracks

I am the weed, unruly and cursed
pushing through the cracks in your pavement
a stubborn green against the hard gray
defying the order of your neat, clean world.
The earth beneath is cracked and broken
yet I rise, inch by inch, in this barren place
my roots clawing for life where no other dares to grow.

In the monotony of your streets, I stand out
a rebel in your midst, wild and unyielding.
Each leaf, a mark of my survival, each stem
a testament to the desperation that drives me.
You cast your gaze, full of scorn, upon me
an unwanted intruder, a blemish on your path.
Yet still, I rise, fierce and untamed
a whisper of life breaking through concrete.

You try to pull me out, to uproot
the chaos I bring, but I return stronger
relentless in my defiance, unbroken
by the curse we were all born under.
I grow wild in the cracks, unbound
a symbol of the curse, and the weeds
that flourish where no one tends to care.

But in all my rebellion, here's the truth
without Him, I am nothing but a weed
lost and wild, feeding on the dry earth.
But God, in His mercy, reached down
and took this unruly stem in His hand.
Through His Son, I was grafted into His love
no longer cursed, no longer wild.

Now I bloom where I once defied
no longer a symbol of rebellion
but a living testament to grace.
The cracks that held me are healed
in His light, and I grow not in spite
of this world, but through Him
a new creation, rooted in His love
a witness to what He can make whole.

In His hands, the cracks are mended
and I rise, not in defiance, but in hope
a tender green, reaching toward the sky
a living proof that with Jesus
even the wildest weed can be redeemed.

The Harvest of the Heart

The leaves flare gold, then burn to red
edges curling in the breath of morning
as if the world, with a brush of fire
paints over what was, to reveal something new.
There's wisdom in the way the trees let go
releasing each leaf with grace
a quiet surrender to the will of the wind.
Nothing holds forever, not even the oak
whose roots know the earth but bow to time.

I walk beneath the fading canopy
the ground a tapestry of brittle memories
each step crunching through what was.
The air hints of winter's approach
but for now, it is autumn's richness
the scent of burning wood, the bite of apples
the slow turn of the world toward stillness.
In this season of letting go, I feel the pull
God's hand working within, stripping the old
the worn, the brittle from my heart.

Like the trees, I release what no longer holds
what I thought would last but was never meant to stay.
He paints my soul with hues unseen
deep strokes of grace, of renewal.
The shedding of the past
though painful, is beautiful
a surrender to the One who knows the seasons
of my heart far better than I ever could.

Each leaf falls in its time, a quiet offering
a testament to the gentle work of His love.
The wind, like a breath of hope

whispers through the branches
of change, of promise, of a heart made new
in the stillness of this season
where the old falls away
and the new is born
rooted in His unchanging grace.

Beneath the Snow

Beneath a quilt of white, the world lies still
each sound muffled, each breath a plume.
Winter, like a long-held breath
settles deep into the earth's bones
and in the silence, the promise begins to stir.

The trees stand tall, their limbs etched in frost
each branch a prayer, reaching up toward the sky
waiting, as we must, for warmth to return
for the breath of spring to whisper through the cold.

In this quiet, patience grows
for winter does not hurry
it reshapes the world slowly
with each snowflake that falls
with each slow turn of light across the sky.

And as the fields lie fallow beneath their frozen blanket
seeds of tomorrow's bloom are cradled in the dark
resting, not forgotten—waiting
for the moment when the ice will melt
and the earth will sing with life again.

So it is with faith—God's timing, like winter
Requires patience, and we must trust
in the quiet work of His hands.
For beneath the snow, something beautiful is growing
a promise of what is yet to be.

And as I walk through this winter world
each step a reminder that all things have their season
I feel the weight of His patience
the quiet unfolding of His plan.
Though the cold seeps into my bones

I know the thaw will come
and with it, the bloom of new life
the work of His hands revealed
in the warmth of a new dawn.

In that light, I will see it all
the beauty born in winter's wait
the faith that endures
and the hope In Jesus
that carries us through.

Guided by Heaven's Light

The night spreads wide, a velvet expanse
where shadows settle into their quiet corners
and stars emerge, distant and steady
whispering ancient truths across the dark.

Each light, a beacon in the stillness
calls out to something deep within
reminding me how small I am
yet how bold my heart can be
standing here beneath this endless sky.

I feel the presence of something greater
a brush of divinity across my soul
guiding me in ways no words can teach
shaping paths that only faith can follow.

No one owns these stars
no one controls their gentle glow.
But in their light, I've come to understand
something of the vastness of God's wisdom
something of His power that reaches beyond the night.

The constellations stretch above me
quiet and certain, mapping out the sky
and I remember
as they remain unshaken, so does His love
holding me in every place, in every step.

Beneath these stars, I find my way
a pilgrim moving through the darkness
trusting the light that surrounds me
trusting the One who placed it there.

And in this quiet, in this space of awe

I feel the pull of His hand
guiding me through the shadows
inviting me to see His presence
in every flicker of light, in every breath of the night.

The road is long, the darkness deep
but these stars speak of something more
something that carries me beyond the moment
a faith that endures, a love that holds steady
guiding me ever onward.

The Last Days of Summer

In these final breaths of summer, the sunlight lingers a little longer
stretching itself across the golden fields
where shadows whisper their secrets to the cooling earth
and the Creator's hand guides each beam
each shadow, reminding me of His steady presence.

Mornings arrive with a crispness now, the kind that nips at your skin
whispering that change is in the air, as God's seasons shift with purpose.
Afternoons still hold their warmth, a gentle embrace before a long journey
each ray a tender farewell
a reminder of the warmth of His love that never fades.

The cicadas' song grows softer, a fading melody that once filled
humid nights with life, now a gentle hum—like the distant memory
of a loved one's voice, echoing in the quiet corners of your mind
and I am reminded of the peace that surpasses all understanding.

I sit on the porch, watching leaves begin to blush with autumn's promise
each one a reminder of time's relentless march
yet also of God's eternal promise.
The garden's blooms are waning, their vibrant hues dulled
yet their beauty remains, a testament to the enduring work of His hands.

Children's laughter drifts through the open window, a chorus of innocence
to be swallowed by school bells and busy streets
yet I know that God's joy remains.
I sip my coffee, savoring the moment, knowing these days are fleeting
like fireflies in a jar, their light fading with dawn, yet His light never dims.

There's a certain peace in this transition
a soft acceptance of what's to come.
The last days of summer are a gentle teacher, whispering in the language
of endings and beginnings
of holding on and letting go

of memories made and dreams yet to be chased
and I see God's hand in each moment, guiding, holding, comforting.

So, as the days grow shorter and the nights a bit longer
I bow my head in quiet prayer, seeking solace in the simplicity of it all
in the quietude that settles like dew on the morning grass.
Lord, guide me through the changes to come
help me to embrace each new beginning
to hold fast to Your truth as I walk this path, knowing that every ending
is but a prelude to the grace of Your new dawn, where Your love and light lead me home.

The Hollow Chase

The world whispers in my ear, a seductive murmur
insisting that I must feel something good all the time.
Such lies, woven from threads of lust, of flesh
of the eyes, of the pride of life
they drain the essence of me
leaving nothing but a hollow shell.

They offer a promise, empty as the wind
this good feeling I'm told to chase
a vapor in the daylight, slipping through my fingers
a specter I can never hold.
Life slips away in an unbearable blur
and they say, perhaps a good feeling will make it bearable.

Moments of fleeting joy, mere fragments of light
in the shadowed corners of my mind.
They say it's enough, but the emptiness gnaws
a beast within, relentless, devouring the core of me.

The eyes crave only what cannot satisfy
the flesh yearns for more, always more
and the pride—oh, the pride—stands tall
casting shadows long and cold
draining the warmth from my soul
leaving me hollow and lost.

Life's weight presses down, unbearable
crushing hope under its merciless heel
leaving me gasping for air, for light
for anything to remind me I am still here
still breathing, still alive.

Yet in the shadows, I search
the world's promises echoing hollow

a haunting chorus in the cavern of my soul
a void unfilled, a thirst unquenchable
a hunger that gnaws within.

But then—a light, not of this world
pierces through the dark
God's Word, steadfast and unyielding
shines like a beacon.
In His truth, the emptiness is driven out
the shadows flee, and the hollow promises of the world
dissolve in the light of grace.

No longer do I chase the fleeting mirage
for in His Word, I find a peace that calms the restless waves
a tranquility that fills the once-empty void.
In Christ, I breathe deep the air of freedom
no longer gasping in the suffocating darkness.
His embrace guides me home
where the lies of the world cannot follow
where peace reigns eternal
and the hollow chase ends in the fullness of His love.

The Creak of Existence

Sitting on the porch, the scent of fresh-cut grass
clings to the heavy air, a green specter
of life, of growth, beneath the relentless sun.
The swing creaks beneath him, each rhythmic sway
a lament for the day's toil, each wooden groan
a song of the body's endurance.

He wipes the sweat from his face, beads of salt
carving paths of effort spent under a sky
that burns with the cruelty of midsummer.
His shirt, soaked through, clings to him
a second skin burdened by the weight
of this brutal day, a testament to survival.

The creak of the swing merges with the cicadas' drone
a monotonous chant against the backdrop
of oppressive heat and stifling humidity.
Time drags, languid and heavy, each second
oozing like the sweat from his brow
each minute a quiet battle.

The grass, freshly cut, lies in perfect rows
a mosaic of labor, green whispers of rest
yet fleeting, mocking the day's merciless heat.
In this narrow moment, the world shrinks to the porch
to the swing, to the man and his silent struggle.

He sits, bandana wiping his face, the swing's creak
an echo to his ragged breaths, as he contemplates
the weight of this day. In the smell of grass
and the sun's relentless gaze, he finds
a connection forged in sweat, each second
a testament to enduring, to existing.

But in the calm of the moment, in the rhythm of the swing
there is more than just struggle—there is strength
not born of his own will, but of faith.
The suffocating humidity, the groan of wood
his salt-streaked face—they whisper truths
about the endurance found not in man alone
but in the grace of God, in Jesus.

And in this quiet perseverance, he finds peace
for it is not by his own strength that he endures
but through the resilience of a faith sustained
by the unfailing love of God.
In Christ, he is carried through
each burden lifted, each trial met
with the quiet assurance of divine grace.

Frost

The frost creeps in, a quiet thief in the night
stealing warmth from the earth, laying bare
a landscape once alive, now frozen, stark.
It is not sudden, this chill—it arrives slowly
unnoticed until one morning you wake
to find the world wrapped in a shroud of ice
still and silent, as if holding its breath.

The air hangs heavy with a silence
that speaks of forgotten dreams
of hopes tucked away in the heart's
deepest, coldest corners. I walk through this winter
each step a reminder of the weight I carry
burdens grown heavier with each passing season.

The cold seeps into my bones, an ache that numbs
dulling the senses, chilling the soul.
Yet even in this desolate stillness
there is a whisper, soft and sure
rising from beneath the frost, telling me
this is not the end.

For in the heart of winter, beneath the ice and snow
life waits, patient, enduring
holding on to the promise of spring.
It is a gradual thing, this return of warmth
not a sudden blaze, but a slow, steady thaw
as the sun's rays break through the clouds
bringing with them the promise of renewal
of rebirth, of a world made new.

And so it is with faith—
not always a roaring fire, but a quiet ember

burning steadily beneath the surface
providing warmth in the coldest of times
a beacon in the darkest night.

This faith sustains me, carries me through the long winter
guiding me gently toward the dawn
where the frost will melt away
and the world, in the light of His grace
will be born anew.

Morning's Promise

Shards of light from the horizon pierce the sky
as the remnants of night slip quietly away
its dark shadows and the doubts they carried
retreating with the dawn. The sun, steady and sure
ascends as clouds gather in silent praise
their edges brushed with hues of purple
and magenta, soft yet steadfast in their embrace.

The night, with its whispers of uncertainty
fades into the folds of memory, a distant echo.
I watch as the first rays cut through the mist
transforming the world with their gentle persistence
each shard a promise, a whisper of hope
painting the sky with strokes of God's faithfulness.

The clouds, like faithful witnesses, gather
to bear testimony to this divine rebirth
their edges glowing with the first light of day
a tapestry woven with threads of grace.
In this moment, the sky holds its breath
honoring the departure of darkness
welcoming the reign of the true light.

I stand, a quiet observer, feeling the warmth
of the sun's embrace, the gentle nudge
against the lingering shadows within.
The light, in all its brilliance, seeps
into the cracks of doubt, filling the voids
left by the night that lingered too long
a reflection of Jesus' light entering my soul.

The horizon, a canvas of possibility
expands with each passing moment

each hue a reflection of battles fought
of victories claimed in the stillness of dawn.
The sun climbs higher, the colors deepen
a symphony of light and shadow in perfect balance
mirroring the balance of justice and mercy.

In this early morning reverie, I find
a mirror to my own faith journey—the ebb
and flow of hope and despair, the constant
dance of light and dark within.
As the sun rises, so does my spirit
embracing the day with the quiet promise
of resurrection, of mercy, of grace
God's unending faithfulness made new every morning

After the Storm

After a night of rain and wind
the lake's storm-tossed waters have found their calm.
I dip my hands into the stirred waters
letting the cold drippings fall
echoes of chaos, reminders of pain.
The water whispers its story in silence
chilling my tongue, settling in my bones
a tale of turmoil now at rest.

The surface, now smooth, mirrors the sky
reflecting the quiet after the tempest
a peace that holds the remnants of struggle
the residue of night's unrest beneath its still calm.
Each drop that slips through my fingers
carries a fragment of the storm's fury
a bitter reminder of battles fought in silence.

In the morning light, the lake reveals its scars
branches torn and adrift
leaves scattered like lost memories.
Yet beneath the surface, life stirs
an undercurrent of resilience
a promise of renewal, of rebirth waiting to rise.
In this quiet, I see the reflection of my own journey
the storms weathered, the chaos tasted, endured.
I drink from the lake, embrace the cold
feeling the whispers within
a testament to the peace found in the aftermath.

But deeper still, I am drawn into a peace profound
a steady calm that holds through every storm.
For in the heart of the tempest, I am anchored
in the unchanging hand of God.

His promises, my shelter through every wind and wave
in Him, I stand secure
not just in the calm but in the storm itself
knowing that in His grace
I am held, I am safe, I am at peace.

Silence of Snow

As night deepens, I pause
the December moon, a steady sentinel
casts its silver touch on a world made new
by ice, cold, and snow.
I gaze upon the field, serene in moonlight
soft, gentle, and pure
a silence so deep it lulls the heart to rest.
The stars whisper in a language only the night understands
their light delicate, like frost on a leaf.
The air, crisp and biting, refreshes the spirit
while the world, wrapped in quiet
waits, suspended in the breath of night.
In the moon's embrace, the snow glistens
each flake a tender reflection of the stillness
a blanket of peace laid upon the earth
inviting the mind to settle, the soul to breathe.
I stand, lost in this moment of calm
the field before me a canvas of dreams
untouched, unmarked, promising
a new day, yet to be painted by the dawn.
Snow silence wraps around my thoughts
easing the weight of the day,
melting fears into the simple clarity of light on white
a reminder of quiet strength within.
I linger at the window
one last look at the field, the snow
the December moon watching overall.
In its gentle light, I find a tranquil peace
a moment of grace that prepares me for the night

with quiet gratitude for the stillness
ready to face the coming day anew.

Moonlit

The frost settles like a memory, cold and thick
covering the earth with what I've held onto
each frozen breath a moment delayed
waiting for the warmth of dawn to thaw the past
and stir what's been buried into light.

For so long, I've clung to these fragments
holding tight to frozen moments
unspoken words lingering on my lips
afraid to let go
to release the weight of dreams that never woke.

Fog rises from the creek, a dragon's tail unfurling
curling through the trees like the past's grip
its tendrils thick with secrets
I've tried to forget but can't.
Each breath of mist a reminder
of what I can't undo
the shadows of choices made
stretching long into the present.

The frost whispers of nights I've spent alone
memories sharp as crystal
each one reflecting pieces of a self I thought I knew
or wanted to know
now blurred in the fog of what was
paths taken and abandoned
leading nowhere I can find again.

In the stillness, I sift through the silence
each shard of the past cutting deep
its power lingering in the quiet.
The moon hangs above, unblinking,

its light a witness to my undoing,
as I trace the lines of what remains
and what I've yet to release.

But here, in this frozen landscape
I begin to see the strength in letting go.
The past may be unyielding
but within its cold grip, I find a quiet grace
a refining fire beneath the surface
a warmth that sustains even in the coldest night.

The frost glimmers like a pearl on the ground
a reminder of what's been deferred but not lost.
In the quiet of this moonlit stillness
a spark of hope ignites
for I know that in the hands of God
the past is not a chain but a chisel
carving the shape of what's to come
etching grace into the fabric of my life.

Now, with my heart rooted in Christ
I stand at peace with what has been
strengthened to face what lies ahead.
The past no longer binds, but teaches
and though unchanging, it changes me.
In His hands, every frozen moment thaws
making way for the path He's laid before me
where every step is firm, every future bright
lit by the unchanging light of His love.

The Warmth of Heaven

Jesus, you left the silk curtains of eternity
the breath of angels' wings still warm, their hum
woven into the fabric of your name. Before flesh
touched you, you were heaven's heartbeat
yet you descended—oh, the plunge—past stars
that know your voice, past galaxies echoing
your glory. What did you wear when time
wrapped you tight? Not robes of majesty
but skin, fragile, taut, carrying the ache
of hunger, the thirst that tightens the throat.

In heaven's corridors, your riches could flood
universes, yet you chose the dust
chose feet that stumbled on stone.
You left it all behind—the light, the throne
the crown gleaming with eternity
to walk our earth, where sin clings to heart
and rebellion cradles us in its arms. Still
you came, eyes set on the horizon
where the cross waited, cold as nails
the warmth of celestial embrace traded
for a kiss of death.

In a single breath, you let go
of the glory of your name, clothed yourself
in mortality, less than angels. Did the stars blink
when you folded your divinity
into our brokenness? Did heaven sigh
when you became the lamb, stepping
toward slaughter, silent, knowing?

You left the Father's side, tasted death
so we might taste life. The glory you laid aside

didn't vanish; it sank into the grain of wood
into the touch of miracles. We felt it, didn't we?
In the way you let women kneel
their tears washing your feet, their hands
touching the hem of something holy.

I wonder if heaven gasped
when You cried out on that cross
when God tasted sin's bitter weight
In that moment
you were alone, the Father's face turned
so that our redemption would be a reality.

What you left behind, you reclaimed
but not without scars. The light you set down
burns now in our bones, a holy fire.
Yet I imagine, even in glory
those wounds still linger
the only trace of earth in heaven
marks that remind us
of the dust you loved enough to wear.

The Anatomy of Pain

This body—fragile, brittle
its bones hollowed by years
by battles unnamed, yet constant
as if life's very gears grind too loud
time swells with pain
each second stretched and torn.

Limbs, once vessels of purpose
curl inward, like branches sealed in frost.
Hands, alive with words once
now falter, stiff as clay
unable to shape the truths
that once poured freely.
And here, the soul watches
as the body becomes shadow.

Doctors stand in rows
armed with tools and sterile knowledge
measuring failure: nerve, sinew, bone.
But where is hope in their cold diagnosis?
The laughter that rises
is brittle, cracking like dead leaves
pressed beneath the weight of unspoken prayers.

If only healing could be carved from flesh
pain peeled away like a riverbed stone
polished smooth by time and distance.
Yet fear keeps the blade from cutting
too deep, too close to the heart.

The world shrinks to a bed
the ceiling pressing in
the body wrestling in silence.
Does heaven listen still

or does God sit with closed hands
as pain fills the air?
The cry of the broken
lost in a language too old to translate.

Yet, through the hollow
something stirs—small, fragile
a whisper not extinguished.
Hope begins to stretch
like roots beneath winter's frozen earth
seeking the unseen light.

Here is the promise
that even in brokenness
there is more
not a world free of ache
but grace that meets us
where the world frays.
A hand, scarred by nails
reaches through the storm
offering not relief alone
but redemption.

For in Christ, every wound bends toward healing
each scar becomes a line in the story
of love that overcomes.
We are not our pain,
not the weight of sorrow.

He is the Savior who bears our weight
lifting what we cannot bear
offering not mere endurance
but a light that guides us into grace.

In Every Quiet Moment

Out here, where the world forgets to look
faith takes root in furrows dark as the hands that tend them.
Corn bends to the wind
its stalks like prayers whispered to the heavens.
The sky listens—vast, patient
and the earth beneath, rich with the weight of seasons
holds each seed like a promise.

They say there's no meaning in the mundane
but I've seen grace in the lifting of bread
in hands rough with work, yet tender with love.
Here, silence holds more weight than words
the quiet acknowledgment that love
like bread, is best when shared.

In the sweat that glistens on backs bent to the soil
I've seen God.
Not in the parting of seas or the shaking of mountains
but in the rhythm of daily toil
in the furrowed brows of men
who keep the world turning
one harvest at a time.

I used to think God spoke only in grand gestures
but His voice is softer here
in the hum of bees, the rustle of leaves
the steady beat of a heart content in the ordinary.
He's in the barn door's creak
the smell of rain after a long dry spell
in the sunset's slow burn across forgotten fields.

We live in the heart of the heart of life
where each moment is stitched into eternity

with threads of quiet grace.
If you've got the eyes to see it
you'll find Him
in the folds of a day well-spent
in the simple miracle of small things.

And isn't that the real miracle?
Finding God not in the storm
but in the breeze that comes after
in the hands folded in prayer over a meal
in the love that lingers in the cracks of our daily lives.
He is here, always here
in the light that returns after rain
in every breath we take without thinking
in the quiet grace of a life lived in service
to the One who makes all things holy.

The Forger's Surrender

I pressed my hands to the canvas
but the colors were not mine
they belonged to others, long gone
whose truths I stole with trembling fingers.
Each brushstroke felt like theft
a lie crafted in oil and light
the work of a man who never prayed.

I moved through galleries of praise
but their applause never touched me.
I was the ghost in the frame
a hollow figure of imitation
pretending at genius but knowing
there was no pulse behind the paint.

The cracks didn't show in the art
but in me, splitting open from the inside.
Each counterfeit was a weight I carried
pulling at the seams of a faith
I no longer knew how to hold.
The image of God I once chased
now buried beneath the layers of paint
I used to hide from the truth.

I thought I could build a monument
from borrowed brilliance
trade the weight of truth for gold
but the price of applause is a hollow currency
and the gilded frames turned to dust
in the hands of strangers who knew nothing
of the ache that stretched behind my smiles.

The praise turned bitter

ash on my tongue, and I knew
nothing I made would stand
when the fire came to test it.
My hands had never been my own
I was merely the forger, the thief
chasing the fleeting light of false glories.

And God? He was never in those forgeries
never in the shining canvases I built
to mask the deepening cracks in my heart.
He waited in the ruin of my pride
in the collapse of the kingdom I built
with hands stained by my own ambition.

Now, as I lay down my brushes
I see the truth I ran from for so long
the masterpiece was never mine to create.
It was His hand all along
waiting to shape something real from the wreckage.

I lay my forgeries at His feet
and in my surrender, I find a grace
I never knew I needed.
He takes the cracks, the flaws
the hollow places where shame once lived
and paints a truth that breathes life.

Now I see, it was never about
the strokes I could lay down for praise.
Only what He builds through me will stand.
Only His truth, carved into the lines of my life
will endure the fire and remain.

Beyond the Glitter

I pressed my hands to the things that sparkle
hoping the shine would make me feel more
more than dust, more than breath held together
by a life that glows only in the light of others' eyes.
But what is gold when the heart feels thin
when the soul wears away under the weight
of what can never fill it?

I've seen houses built like temples
polished to impress, gleaming with perfection,
but behind every door, there's silence too thick to breathe
and rooms too perfect to be lived in.
The shine fades quickly when no one's there
to truly see you, beyond the glitter and the gloss.

Jesus never draped Himself in wealth
He bore no crown of gold but one of thorns.
His hands, rough from lifting the broken
held no coin but carried the weight of a cross
heavy with the world's sorrow
yet lightened by love only He could offer.

And yet, we forget.
We chase what reflects in glass
instead of what shines in our hearts.
But no gleam compares to the quiet peace
of knowing who we are—loved, redeemed
by the One who needed no wealth to show us our worth.

What good is a treasure locked in a room
when the real gold lies in the hands that give?
Let the glitter fall to dust, let it scatter to the winds
for the wealth we seek is not in things
but in the heart that knows where it belongs.

I have seen it now
our worth was never in the gold we gathered
but in the love we give away
in the hands of a Savior who saw beyond the shine
to the soul that needed saving.

Search for Light

One walks through the endless corridors of thought
lined with books whispering theories, brittle pages
attempting to explain the world, piece by piece
yet meaning unravels, lost in the spaces between questions.

In rooms where shadows lengthen like doubts
philosophy builds its towers of sand, too fragile
for restless souls seeking a place to set down
the heavy weight of all they do not know.
Answers slip through like water, leaving the weight behind.

They reach for wisdom in the earth's bones
for truth in stars that flicker, but speak nothing.
Sifting through the dust of reason
they search for something solid to fill
the hollow places doubt has carved
but each path leads back to the same void
every answer curling inward, unfinished, fading.

And in the silence that follows, as not knowing grows heavy
a voice breaks through—not from books, nor stars
but from the cross, where meaning was born
where truth does not fade. Christ's voice does not echo back emptiness
his words hold fast while all else crumbles to dust.

What is peace, if not a heart bound to Jesus?
What is meaning, but the breath He gives
a life unfolding not toward the empty winds of the world
but to the fullness of His grace, filling the hollow
bringing light where shadows once claimed the mind.

They believed the world held answers
that within its labyrinth of thought lay a thread
to lead them out. But the thread was not theirs to hold

it was His hand, scarred and reaching down
writing truth across a wandering heart.

In Christ, the search finds its end.
The restless mind rests, the questions settle.
They sought meaning in the world's broken lights
but in His face, they find the reflection
of what they were made to be
a soul known and loved, no longer searching.

Where Light Begins

The path was never gentle
we stumbled, stones digging deep into our skin
each burden heavier than the words we never spoke.
Grief carved its lines across our hearts
sharp as glass pressed into flesh
our voices lost in the echo of everything that broke us.
We carried it all, this weight
as if it could somehow tell us who we were
as if pain was the author to write our name.

But here, where the world softens
and the sky begins to breathe light again
there is more than wreckage
more than the shadows we walked through.
It is not the sorrow that holds us now
and it was never the dark that claimed us.

Even in the deepest silence
a voice calls—not to erase the hurt
but to lift the weight that buried us.
The promise was never that suffering would disappear
but that grace would meet us in the hollow places
filling what we thought could never be made whole.

What is this grace but hands scarred by nails
reaching through every chaotic storm.
A mercy that stands firm, even as the world crumbles.
Here, in Christ, we are not forgotten
we are not lost.
We are held in the hands of Jesus
who knew the weight we carried
and bore it for us.

In Jesus, every broken piece turns toward light
every scar becomes a story of redemption.
What was once our wound
is now the place His love has healed.

This is not the end of the journey
it is the beginning
where everything reaches for wholeness
where pain is not the final word.
We are more than what broke us
more than the shadows that once
swallowed our steps.
We are seen, we are loved
and in His grace, we rise—made new.

Let our hearts remember this
it is not the grief and pain that defines us
but the Savior who carried us through.
And in His hands, the weight we once bore
becomes the light that guides us home.

Afterword

Engaging in Reflection

As you close this collection of poems, I invite you to pause in this moment of stillness. These poems have taken us through seasons of grief and grace, sorrow and hope—each one a reflection of our shared journey in life. You may have found echoes of your own story in these pages, moments where the words touched your heart, stirred your soul, or challenged your faith.

Now, in the quiet, let this be a time to reflect on what God is speaking to you. Consider the journey you've walked through these poems—one of pain, healing, and, ultimately, the resilient grace found in Jesus Christ. Take this time not merely as a conclusion, but as an invitation to go deeper in your own reflections and to listen for the whisper of God's voice in the midst of your story. Let these questions guide you as you reflect on how His grace has carried you through your own storms.

1. Where has God carried me in my struggles?

    In life's hardest moments, God's hand is often unseen, yet He is always there. Reflect on a particular hardship where you later recognized God's presence, His comfort, or His provision—even when it felt absent. How does that change the way you view your current struggles?

    Read: Isaiah 41:10, Romans 8:28, Psalm 46:1–3

2. How has God's peace sustained me through chaos?

    There are times when life feels overwhelming, and yet, God offers a peace that defies our circumstances. Think back to moments when that peace took hold of you—when fear was replaced by calm, even though nothing around you changed. How can you seek that peace again in your present or future challenges?

    Read: Philippians 4:6–7, John 14:27, Isaiah 26:3

3. What has my grief revealed about God's love?

Afterword

Grief has a way of shaping us, but it also brings us nearer to God's heart. Reflect on a time of deep loss—how did God meet you in that place of sorrow? Did His comfort bring you closer to Him, even in your pain? Let this reflection remind you that He walks with us through our darkest valleys.

Read: Psalm 34:18, 2 Corinthians 1:3–4, Revelation 21:4

4. How has God refined my faith through waiting and struggle?

Seasons of waiting can feel endless, but they are often where God does His greatest work. Think about a time of waiting or hardship in your life—how did it shape your trust in God? What lessons did you learn about His timing that continue to impact your faith today?

Read: Isaiah 40:31, Lamentations 3:25–26, Psalm 27:14

5. How can I become more aware of God's presence in my daily life?

God is present in every moment, but we often miss Him amid the noise of life. Reflect on your daily habits—are there places where you can create space to notice God more? What changes can you make to live with greater awareness of His presence, even in the small, ordinary moments?

Read: Psalm 139:7–10, James 4:8, Colossians 3:17

In these reflections, may you be reminded that God's grace is woven through every part of your story—through your joy, your pain, and your healing. Whether you're grieving old wounds, waiting in uncertainty, or discovering the depths of His faithfulness, God is there, guiding you toward hope and restoration.

And at the heart of it all is Christ. The ultimate expression of God's grace and mercy is found in Jesus, the One who carries us through every trial and offers us not just survival but abundant life. If you have yet to receive this gift of grace, Jesus invites you to know Him—His forgiveness, peace, and the new life found in His sacrifice and resurrection. Read: Romans 10:9–10.

Let this time of reflection be honest and open. Whether you are walking with Christ, seeking Him more deeply, or on the edge of a new understanding, know that God's love is unending, His grace unshakable, and His presence ever near.

May these reflections bring you nearer to Jesus, who walks with you through every storm, and may God's grace guide you into a deeper encounter with the peace, joy, and love found only in Him.

www.ingramcontent.com/pod-product-compliance
Lightning Source LLC
Chambersburg PA
CBHW061453040426
42450CB00007B/1340